I'm Still
in Here!

Intuitive Assistance for Caregivers
Tending to Those Who Can't Communicate

Louise Platt Hauck

MEDITATION AND AFFIRMATIONS
with Jaene Leonard, iRest® Teacher

Lamplight Publishing Company
New York, New York

ISBN: 978-0-9769205-8-8 (print)
ISBN: 978-1-7360178-2-1 (eBook)

Lamplight Publishing Company
511 6th Avenue, Ste. 234
New York, NY 10011

To Dan and Denise

Jaene Leonard is the perfect collaborator. Her iRest® Meditation expertise integrates beautifully with this book's message. Her intrinsic, intuitive, and compassionate way of blending the metaphysical with the physical has been instrumental in helping to organize and synthesize ideas in this book. She also worked closely with me as I wrote toward simplifying and effectively communicating complex, abstract concepts.

Contents

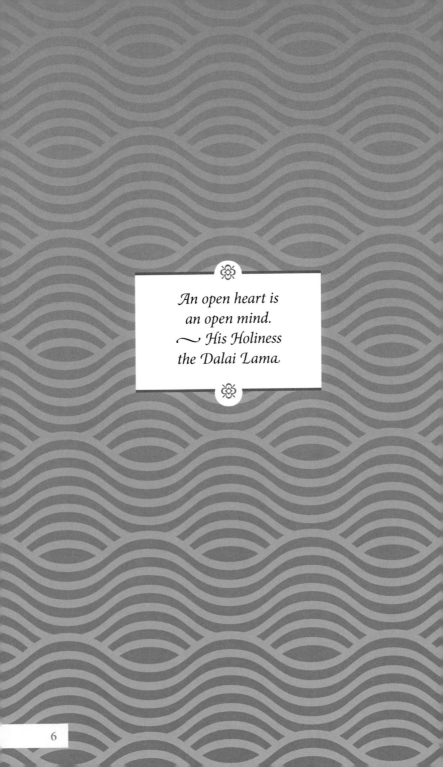

*An open heart is
an open mind.*
~ *His Holiness
the Dalai Lama*

Wholeness

My heart goes out to caregivers — family, friends, and professionals who tend day-to-day to those experiencing the effects of dementia, autism, stroke, coma, and other anomalies that inhibit usual ways of communicating. I honor you. The time and patience required of you can take an emotional and physical toll, and requires superhuman patience. Whether you are in this caregiving role out of love and devotion, professional obligation, or a sense of personal duty, you've been called into extraordinary service that is all-consuming. It can be exhausting.

Part of maintaining your sanity is building resilience, taking a little time to connect to *your own well-being* every day. When you're present, you see things more clearly, and this can lead to epiphanies — sudden intuitive moments of realization.

It also may be helpful to remind yourself that the work before you, though difficult, is honorable work. Take care of yourself and take heart; this challenge isn't forever.

In my work as an intuitive spiritual counselor, I've seen clients like you stretched beyond their limits, dealing with circumstances and responsibilities imposed upon them and leaving little or no room for personal pursuits. Compassion fatigue is considered secondary traumatic stress (STS), so it's important to make time each day, even in small moments, to detach and get present, to better deal with *what is*.

The important thing for you as the caregiver is to be gentle with yourself and stay open to a new way of seeing things. This is where I come in.

I'm able to tune-in to the one being cared for and interpret information telepathically, which helps caregivers reorient to a fresh understanding of what's going on behind the scenes.

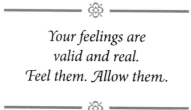

*Your feelings are
valid and real.
Feel them. Allow them.*

Taking a Closer Look

The person you care for may seem like a stranger — or they may treat you like one. They may seem completely absent or vacant. They may be sad, frustrated or full of rage. You, in turn, may feel some of these same feelings. Don't beat yourself up. Your feelings are valid and real. Feel them. You're allowed.

There may be a temptation to see the one cared for as less of a person, as somehow gone from themselves. But, there's another way of seeing that person — *as whole* and operating concurrently on a very unique level of consciousness.

The information I'm sharing here will reposition you and illuminate the dark moments that seem to create a chasm between the two of you.

It's my hope that fostering a new way of looking at things might ease the pressure a bit and quiet an urge you may have to break through, a longing to return to the way things were, or an impulse to give up and phone it in!

This expanded perspective can be very useful for you in your current endeavors. But it will require some things of you.

You'll be asked to examine your personal story and change your perspective about who you are in relation to the person you're tending to. You'll be required to detach from old grievances, conditioning, and expectations that may very possibly *never* be resolved. You must be willing to enter into a new kind of relationship — one you might not have considered before this moment.

If you're receptive to these ideas, you may find yourself in a new world revealing unexpected opportunities to connect. You may gather new memories you will cherish down the road. You may even have fewer regrets when everything is said and done.

Self-Care and Connecting to YOUR Wholeness

We are all so much more than the roles we play. It's essential for your own well-being to keep this in mind. Start factoring in time for self-care. If you're rolling your eyes, know that small, regular increments of self-compassion can be as effective as a day at the spa.

The importance of taking care of yourself during this time cannot be stressed enough. Whether you're serving in this capacity out of love or obligation, it's essential to *build resilience.* It will help strengthen your ability to respond rather than react when things are intense. It will help you sharpen a reflex to return to center when you've felt tossed way out there.

Building resilience will also increase your courage and stamina and open your heart, so you can go the extra mile compassionately when you feel your energy depleted.

Make a promise to yourself RIGHT NOW to connect to your personal wholeness every day — alone, if possible. Don't use up all your precious alone time venting to someone else. (Venting has its place, just not in your self-care time!)

Here are a few suggestions to help fill the compassion tank:

- Meditate.
- *Journal.*
- Attend an online support group.
- Go for a brisk walk.
- Find an online exercise class.
- Check in with a nutritionist to make sure you're staying on track with healthy eating.
- Make a vision board with future goals.

If you're saying, "Louise, I can't take the time!" Fine. I get it.

Do something simple, like —

- Step outside and look around, as though it's all-new.
- Take a relaxing hot bath.
- Watch a movie.
- Find kitty or puppy videos on YouTube.
- Go for a ride in your car and sing your favorite song — *out loud.*

It's a clue that you're not getting enough self-care if you start falling into a martyrdom mentality. Listen to your body and your self-talk. You're receiving hints!

Staying present with who you are is difficult, even under ideal circumstances. It's easy to lose oneself in work, chosen or obligatory. Make a fresh commitment to yourself each day and align with the Universe. Remind yourself you are not alone. The Universe is always with you, supporting you.

The more you connect with your wholeness, the more you'll be able to connect with the wholeness of the one you care for.

You must let go
of how things used to be ⌒
or how you think things
should be.

Your contribution,
believe it or not,
is a gift to
our evolving humanity.

The Caregiver's Corner

This is your Caregiver's Corner — a private place for you to connect with the deep well of support that exists inside you and is in alignment with everything, everyone, always.

Return to this place whenever you need to feel grounded, restored, and present.

With love and compassion,
Jaene

Please accept this short iRest® practice as our gift to you in honor of your service.

www.louisehauck.com/iRestJaene

The Promise

I always have within me the perfect
response to each moment.

I promise to remind myself of this.

When I observe that I'm being reactive, or my
responses are short, I promise to take a minute
away to breathe, lengthening my exhales.

I'll put my hand on my belly and let my belly soften.

With each exhale, I'll think the words, "let
go," knowing I can release my fears.

I can let go of any frustration I feel about my role as
caregiver. I will remind myself that my frustration is
based in fear of the unknown, and this fear is human.

I'll remind myself that the one I tend to
also struggles, and needs compassion.

If I'm unable to get away for a minute, I promise
to observe my breath right where I am.

I'll focus on lengthening my exhales.

I'll focus on my exhales.

I'll focus on the movement of my exhales.

I'll focus on lengthening my exhales.

I'll repeat the words, "let go."

This won't detract from my current duties — in fact,
it will help me focus better and be more present.

The Prayer

Source, please.

Srengthen my patience,

Enhance my compassion,

Fine-tune my capacity to observe.

Help me honor and be mindful of my body
so that I can stay strong and healthy.

Help me to breathe deeply, with nice, long exhales.

Breath is the access point to my patience,
compassion, and ability to observe.

Breath is where I return to mindfulness.

Mindfulness is being fully accepting of
things *as they are*...in each moment.

The Practice

Upon Waking

Bring attention to breath. With each
lengthening exhale, affirm:

I am Whole.

The one I care for is Whole.

I am kind and compassionate.

The Universe is kind and compassionate.

The Universe is expanding.

I am at one with the Universe.

I am present.

I am patient.

I am loved.

I am Love.

In Times of Frustration

Bring attention to breath. With each
lengthening exhale, affirm:

Let go.

I let go of my frustration.

I let go of expectation.

I let go of judgment.

I surrender to the wisdom of the moment.

I am here, now.

I am compassionate.

I am with things as they are right now.

Before sleep

Bring attention to breath. With each
lengthening exhale, affirm:

My work is done for now.

The Universe is kind and compassionate.

The Universe is expanding.

I am one with the Universe.

I am present.

I am patient.

I am loved.

I am Love.

I welcome and now enter into deep, restorative sleep.

Bonus Affirmation

In Moments of Gratitude

I am loved.

My heart is open.

The Universe is abundant and giving.

I am thankful for the gifts.

I am grateful to be part of the mystery.

*"I always ask that
I be a clear facilitator
for the most reliable
and relevant information
that is for your highest good
to receive, and for my
highest good to deliver."*

Louise's
Orientation

A major focus of my work for over thirty years has involved merging with a unifying field, where I communicate with the souls of loved ones who've left this physical dimension and exist now in the non-physical realm. I no longer refer to it as 'death' or 'the other side' because I've come to understand it as a state of consciousness, rather than an ending or *a place*.

In this timeless flow of consciousness, or what I call *Streaming Consciousness*, I access specific information and impressions that override the limitations of the physical self.

This information reflects the expansive nature of consciousness itself, unifying us in a timeless flow of thought that connects everything — including those of us in the physical and our loved ones in the non-physical.

In an unexpected evolution of my lifelong exploration into consciousness, I began using my intuitive abilities to communicate with the Higher-Selves of those still existing in physical form. And here we are!

I came to realize that it makes no difference whether I'm telepathizing with souls in the physical — or *non*-physical — it's all the same in this accessible consciousness stream.

I communicate with those experiencing the effects of dementia, autism, stroke, in a coma, or sustained on life-support — those who cannot communicate verbally or coherently. I've found this particular work is best done remotely (over the phone), given the unavoidable distractions of the physical self and the surrounding environment.

When I communicate telepathically with those who are non-verbal, I receive remarkably detailed information which can beneficially impact their care and comfort.

Nonlocal Consciousness

In 1989, Dr. Larry Dossey coined the term 'nonlocal' consciousness in his book, *Recovering the Soul*. He defines it as "a spatially and temporally infinite aspect of our consciousness. Nonlocal mind resembles the age-old concept of the soul."

I refer to nonlocal consciousness as the Higher-Self. Its remarkable accessibility enables me to communicate with others no matter the restrictions or limitations of the physical self.

I've also used this type of Higher-Self communication to conduct telepathic conversations and facilitate resolution between clients and partners, ex-partners, relatives, friends, co-workers, and employers.

Merging remotely with the Higher-Self—this timeless aspect of another's consciousness—can extend healing beyond the personality-self. This personality-self perceives itself as 'separate' and is often engaged in earthly drama, ego-driven agendas, and karmic cycles of repeating themes.

Another marvelous functionality of Streaming Consciousness is that healing can extend beyond death and through lifetimes.

"*Humbleness, forgiveness,
clarity, and love
are the dynamics of freedom.
They are the foundations
of authentic power.*"
~ *Gary Zukav*

Consultations for Caregivers ～ Merging with Others

I always begin consultations by inviting clients and caregivers to take a deep breath with me to get us 'in sync' and onto the same frequency. I then recite my invocation, affirming our higher purpose in working together:

I always ask that I be a clear facilitator for the most reliable and relevant information that is for your highest good to receive, and for my highest good to deliver. I surround us with the Light — for energy, protection, and to attract good things. I ask that all the information is within God's sight, and according to God's plan for your greater, eternal self.

Once I've set forth this heartfelt intention, I then shift my frequency to one of gratitude, which opens my heart and pulls me into the flow of Streaming Consciousness. Here, I'm able to merge with the Higher-Self of my client where information immediately flows in my direction.

Similar to playing a game of charades, Higher-Selves pantomime for me specific scenes and transmit clear thoughts concerning their needs and preferences, fears, and troublesome issues. They also convey their awareness of moments shared with family members and others around them.

The non-verbal patient often shows me scenes from the past to illustrate their feelings and clarify a present issue they might want to emphasize.

*The distinction between
the past, present, and future
is only a stubbornly
persistent illusion.*
~ *Albert Einstein*

*Higher-Self communication
promotes powerful
resolution in relationships.*

Stories from Consultations

I find it's always helpful to illustrate my work with clients by sharing stories from consultations.

"Your Mother Wants You to Know How It Feels"

A client's 94-year-old mother with dementia was non-verbal and residing in a memory care facility. She was exhibiting combative behavior, an expression of her extreme frustration.

Once merged with her Higher-Self, I felt us reaching out to touch something soft and fuzzy. It was a pleasant sensation, a warm and loving feeling. I reported this to her daughter.

She said the administrator had recently approved visits onsite from an emotional support puppy, allowing him to enter residents' rooms for warmth, affection, and tactile healing.

Still merged, the mother took me with her — beyond time, in Streaming Consciousness — to a moment in her past, a scene depicting her daughter (my client) as a child at four years old. I felt the sensation of tightness around our arms.

"Yes," my client said, "Mother used to sew dresses for me. Sometimes she'd make the elastic in the sleeves too tight!"

I then felt a constricting feeling around my feet.

"Well," I said, "your mother wants you to know that's how she feels when attendants strap her feet to the wheelchair footplates too tightly!"

At the end of these Higher-Self conversations, I always ask the Higher-Self to share with me a sneak preview of what I call a *cosmic wink* — some sort of signal they'll be sending along to the client (or caregiver) in the following days to confirm that our telepathic conversation did, in fact, take place.

They might show me the image of a coin, soon to be spotted on the sidewalk, a bird perched for extended time on the windowsill (or other animals approaching uncharacteristically), or perhaps wind chimes ringing on a windless day.

Here's the confirmation I received from this client:

Hi, Louise! I don't know if I ever shared this story with you. In one of the sessions right after my dad passed 20 years ago, you shared that my dad would be communicating with me through a bird or something about a bird. And you asked if there had been any "close encounters" with birds and told me to keep an eye out for one.

Well, it wasn't until later that I started to recognize what you were talking about. When my dad was passing, I had a few moments alone with him and sang to him the Beatles song, Blackbird. *You know, "Take these broken wings and learn to fly..." The blackbird has shown up over the years since his passing.*

An especially poignant moment happened two years ago when I took my mom out to a resort on Christmas eve after she was already progressing into Alzheimer's. I had never told her about these communications and we were sitting together having dinner when she said to me, "[Your Dad] was telling me today about . . . " She stopped herself and asked me if my dad was still alive.

I said he wasn't, then added, "but that doesn't mean he wasn't talking to you." She said that she could swear that he was with her all day.

I said, "Maybe he came to help us celebrate the holidays!"

Then I decided to tell her for the first time about how he communicates to me at special times through the song "Blackbird" to let me know that he is still around.

Well, as it happens, there was a live musician in the lounge where we were eating, and literally, the next song he played was "Blackbird." She couldn't believe it, and well, I absolutely knew he was there with us that night to help us celebrate the holidays!

Nothing Is Ever Lost

Two daughters reported that their father with dementia could barely talk. What they could understand usually made no sense.

They said that just before his illness took hold he'd begun to open up about his time in the Navy. His ship was 'kamikazed' three times during the attack on Pearl Harbor. The family was beginning to understand he'd been suffering from Post Traumatic Stress since 1941.

I'm usually pretty good at flipping off my intuiting switch when I'm off duty. Occasionally, however, when I'm contemplating an upcoming consultation, I'll open my heart to the one I'll be engaging through our Higher-Selves, and we connect ahead of time. I sensed the father's presence, even before the start of his daughter's scheduled phone session!

The moment I felt him connecting with me, I sent him my thoughts, "Your current state must be incredibly frustrating for you, and for your daughters and all who love you, as well. They pray for your release — when it's your time — and when you've accomplished all you've come here to do in this lifetime.

"They also pray that your upcoming journey, your transition from this physical experience into the non-physical — existing then as pure consciousness — will be a smooth, seamless, and joyful one."

Then I asked, "Is there anything you might be holding onto, anything that might be impeding your eventual 'liftoff'?"

The father showed me two specific items he was holding onto — "the STORIES," and the "GOLD!"

I assured him (with my thoughts) that his stories would remain in the hearts of all who know and love him, but he was still emphatic about "The GOLD!"

When we officially began the session, I asked his daughters about 'the GOLD!' One of his daughters laughed, and then clarified:

"Dad was always envious of his brother-in-law's GOLD Cadillac Coupe DeVille! He had promised it to our father, but our Uncle lived to be 102! Dad always fretted that someone else would get the 'GOLD,' but he did inherit the car.

I assured their father that the car — and his loved ones — would be waiting for him when it was his time. (Our thought-forms go with us and help create our customized 'heaven').

Finally, I telepathized to him a request for a sneak preview of a cosmic wink. He sent me a scene depicting a sudden motion and a deliberate, sustained glance directed at one his daughters.

A short time after the session, one of the daughters emailed me. She reported that following our phone session, she and her sister went to sit at the bedside of their father, as they regularly did.

Some time had passed, when he suddenly sat bolt upright in his bed, looked around, and then focused on one of the daughters, looking straight into her eyes.

"What the HELL has everyone been TALKING about?!" he roared, and then lay back down and closed his eyes.

The daughter reminded me that their Dad had been non-verbal for some time. (This phenomenon is referred to as an 'end-of-life-rally', or 'terminal lucidity' — the abrupt return of mental clarity shortly before death.)

The sisters informed me that their father passed peacefully a few days later.

An Unusual Occurrence

There's a curious thing I experience occasionally before conductiong a consultation with someone who is non-verbal. Curiously, non-verbal clients can 'tune-in' to *me*, even before I begin to do so with them!

I was interpreting for a client's non-verbal autistic daughter in their initial consultation. At the start of our phone session, the young girl projected a panto-mimed gesture, as if she was pointing to me, back to her, then back to me.

I was surprised to receive from her my impression of the word — 'Louise!'

I asked her mother, "Didn't you email me that your daughter's name is LuisA?"

"Yes," she replied. "An unusual thing happened yesterday. Luisa was coloring at her little table when I saw that she had written the name, 'LuisE' — with an 'E' instead of an 'A.' She wrote it several times. She's never done that before!"

"Had you told her that we would be meeting today?" I asked.

"No," she replied.

I interpreted Luisa's gestures to mean that she knew we'd be meeting — sent from her timeless, overseeing Higher-Self.

This example demonstrates the interactive, timeless nature of Higher-Self to Higher-Self communication. Also, where some might perceive those diagnosed with certain anomalies as *less than whole*, this demonstrates that wholeness is the nature of each and every one of us.

Many who have physical or mental challenges in this dimension are highly intuitive and are already operating in expanded consciousness.

I recently received additional, fun confirmation from Luisa's mother regarding the cosmic winks her daughter previewed for us in our session:

"You asked me if my husband made paper airplanes. Turns out, he had just made two for our other daughter out of receipts that morning while waiting at the car wash. It's something he'd never done before.

"You told me that Lu likes to almost skate through mud puddles and probably about 20 minutes before we started our conversation, Luisa had gotten off the bus, literally skated through a mud puddle. I had to throw her shoes out!

"You also told me that Luisa would want to be known for drawing rainbows. I told you that we were so excited that she had just drawn her first one. Well, let me tell you, for the next three months, Lu filled up notebooks with rainbows, every piece of schoolwork that came home had a rainbow on it. She even wore rainbow socks. It was awesome!"

You Can Trust Those Thoughts

Dan is a devoted husband and dedicated caregiver for his beloved wife, Denise, diagnosed with Alzheimer's Disease at the age of fifty-six. She has been in advanced stages and living in a memory care facility for the past four years.

Through the progression of his wife's disease, Dan had come to believe that he and Denise were communicating telepathically. He was reasonably sure they had been communicating this way for some time and searched online for information that would confirm these conversations. He found me online when he did a search for 'connecting with the Higher-Self of another.'

Here's how Dan summarized his situation in his email:

My wife has become increasingly non-verbal, and it is difficult to figure how she needs help. She exhibits crying episodes, as she gets frustrated, trying to do tasks that were previously simple, but now she can't do at all. She is also very aware of where the disease is taking her and cries over that. The doctor recently prescribed an anti-anxiety medication, which has improved her demeanor, and makes life more tolerable and pleasant for her and those of us around her.

The thought came to me from my Higher-Self that I should communicate with Denise's in order to understand her feelings and be better able to help her. I soon realized, however, that the message actually came directly from Denise's H-S. I could sense and feel that the voice I heard was not my own and that instead, it was Denise's H-S that was speaking to me. I am so blessed to have made this direct connection and have subsequently been communicating with her H-S.

I was thrilled to hear from Dan. It had been a dream of mine to show others how to do what I do and trust the thoughts exchanged. When there's heartful and appropriately invited connectivity, telepathy is *not* just a 'woo-woo' phenomenon.

I've been working with apprentices for years, cheering them on, validating, and helping them fine-tune their own special way of intuiting. Dan and Denise brought a new dynamic to my work. I was thrilled to confirm their communication and encourage Dan to keep trusting and developing his unique process.

In Dan's initial session, Denise merged immediately, demonstrating the ease with which she was operating in expanded consciousness. "Yes, Dan," she confirmed, "you *did* catch my thoughts — *the cat needs a bath.*"

Dan signed on as an apprentice, and we worked together over the phone for several months. Ten months following his first session, it came time for me to get on the road for a tour. It worked out conveniently for me to add a stop along the way to visit Dan and Denise.

In our last phone session before my departure, I asked Denise (telepathically) for a sneak preview of a cosmic wink I might receive when we'd finally meet in person. She projected a scene depicting something falling off a counter or some sort of shelf.

By the time of my arrival, Denise's physical condition had deteriorated considerably and didn't match the smart and bubbly gal I'd come to know through Streaming Consciousness.

I had become very well-acquainted with Denise's *whole* self, interacting with her Higher-Self for nearly a year. It was a striking contrast to meet her in person. I was grateful for the opportunity.

I also realized Higher-Self to Higher-Self communications are more effective without physical distractions. Remote meetings are now my preferred protocol.

At lunchtime, we accompanied Denise into the dining hall. She was clearly a favorite of the staff, and I sensed it was mutual when their gentle teasing made her smile.

Denise fed herself, requiring some assistance at times. Her tray was cleared, and fresh-baked chocolate chip cookies were set out on the counter behind our table. I turned in my chair to check out the desert that smelled wonderful.

Before I turned all the way around, a plate with one of the large cookies slid off the counter and fell to the floor, cookie and plate landing upside down with a loud bang.

I looked at Denise, and she looked back and smiled. This incident was the cosmic wink she had previewed for me in our chat weeks before!

I said to Dan, "There's the cosmic wink!"

A Closed Door

A client signed up for a session, emailing me that she needed guidance. She and her brother were solely responsible for their mother, who'd been diagnosed with dementia.

Her mother had become belligerent while residing at a nearby facility and had made several attempts to leave. Unfortunately, the staff wasn't equipped to deal with runaways, and the client and her brother had to remove her.

They relocated her to another care facility four hours away. The daughter worked full-time but did her best to visit as often as she could.

Over the holidays, she visited and brought her mother a stuffed animal, a cuddly little monkey as a Christmas gift. She said, "The minute I walked through the door, Mom looked like she wanted to KILL me. I delivered her gift and left."

The daughter and her brother considered moving their mother back to the closer facility, now better equipped to care for her. But they were concerned about the stress it might cause her.

Merging with the Higher-Self of another is usually effortless for me. We come together on a higher frequency to communicate without resistance or negative influences from the limited personality-self.

This time, however, the moment I felt connected to the mother, I suddenly sensed a SLAM, as if she'd shut the door in my face! The Higher-Self usually operates separately from and beyond the personality. But this personality-self was far-reaching and very resistant to merging!

It was the first time I'd ever experienced such hostility, and it also gave me a new understanding of how it must feel for so many of you caregivers when you reach out with good intentions and get shut out.

I continued to hold the space of unconditional love and acceptance, and then, suddenly, it seemed as though the door opened just a crack. I felt a connection.

I took the opportunity to send Mom the thought-message, "Your son and daughter love you very much. They want to do what's best for you, but they need your help."

I received back the sensation of a fuzzy toy. I interpreted this as an acknowledgment of the gift her daughter delivered and that she appreciated the Christmas gift.

I continued, "They need to know how you'd feel about moving you back to the other facility where you stayed before."

Then I experienced a new sensation. It was the sound-and-smell of GREEN. This is a sensory phenomenon referred to as synesthesia, a condition where people experience the senses crossing:

Synesthetes often 'see' music as colors, (as the singer Pharrell Willams has described). Other synesthetes might 'taste' textures like 'round' or 'pointy' when they eat foods. My synesthetic friend once told me, "Last Thursday tasted so almond!"

My client thought for a moment when I reported receiving the sensation of 'green' from her mother.

"Oh, right!" she exclaimed, " Mother did enjoy walking in the beautiful garden at that first facility. Do you think she's giving us a 'thumbs-up?'"

I said, "She's remembering what she liked about her stay there, so yes, I'm interpreting that as a thumbs up!"

We often telepathize with each others unknowingly.

Accessing Connectivity by Shifting Your Frequency

Two Powerful Tools

Here are a couple of ways to help you get on the same frequency and connect with the one you care for.

TOOL #1: REFRAMING

Reframing your caregiving situation can lead to seismic shifts in your relationship, and how you relate to each other.

Simple renaming a problem a *challenge* might help you muster courage and tap into creative challenge-solving. Taking another look and seeing things from a different angle can promote new understanding.

Another powerful way to reframe is to take a step back, especially when emotions are flaring. Doing so will allow you to put things on pause and reflect for a moment. Revisit the Caregiver's Corner for some focus and affirmations (page 16).

When you reframe, you might be pleasantly surprised at the subtle cues and discernible responses you'll receive back from that person you're seeing as whole — moments of lucidity or clarity, quick, loving gestures, or other meaningful signals. As you begin to trust more signals, you'll receive all the more confirmation.

As difficult as it might be to make an effort to connect with the heart and see wholeness in the one you're caring for, it's worth a try. And it's worth it to keep trying. Why?

Reframing helps you perceive the other as a unique individual who's contending with earthly challenges like the rest of us. You might be less inclined to confine their identity to a character in your story, "My mother with Alzheimer's," or "Dad . . . ever since the stroke", or such depersonalizing references as "that patient who's out of her mind."

The things that are driving you crazy will eventually fall away. In the way that we reminisce about grandparents, former partners, friends, pets — all those we've loved and lost through the years — you'll eventually recall the best of the one you care for.

Also, you'll come to understand that just like you, they are very complex beings, operating on more than the most observable level of consciousness. Through Streaming Consciousness, we connect on the level of the Higher-Self.

Thoughts and feelings transmit through the airwaves. We often telepathize with each other unknowingly.

As you start to become more conscious and work to reframe your situation, you'll begin to experience a new level of connectivity.

Moments When You've Felt the Love
(Another Way to Reframe)

A client booked a reading out of concern for her mother for whom she'd been caring, one way or another, all her life. In recent years, it had become a full-time job because her mother was experiencing intermittent periods of dementia. The client was angry and exhausted.

She said of the many nurses assisting her along the way, "They all hate Mom, and she hates all of us, too! She has ousted every medical person and hired and fired at least sixty caregivers."

The mother had exhibited extremely combative behavior for quite some time, scoffing and yelling at everyone who tried their best to assist her.

When I merged with her Higher-Self, I experienced the soothing sensation that often indicates there's a pet nearby. This time it felt smoother and silkier than that of a cuddly pup or kitten.

"Yes," the client replied, "Mom likes it when we bring in one of her two geese for her to pet! Outside there's a camera pointed at their pen so she can watch them on her TV monitor."

"So, it's clear that your mother responds to tenderness," I said. There was silence on the phone.

I could tell the daughter was still having trouble relating to her mother in this way. So I tried a different approach.

"Might there be a photo of your mother," I asked, "one which might connect to some singular moment — just one — when you felt love for each other?" I was shown the example of a loving moment, the scene of a cart . . . and a pig . . . I asked her about it.

"Well . . ." she said, "maybe there's ONE . . . it's a photo on her nightstand, behind some others."

I asked if she could pull out that photo and look at it, then try to bring back the feeling of that rare moment of love exchanged between them when their hearts were open.

I felt the client was having trouble accessing feelings of tenderness toward her mother.

"I guess I have a lot of work to do," she said. I heard some sadness in her voice, but I knew we were on the right track. Simple observation of one's actions and emotions can begin to shift things in incredible ways.

"Well, what if I told you," I said, "that all the negativity you and others feel for your mother is keeping her here? Even though it's not a joyous connection and is unbearably unpleasant for all of you — it's still a form of connectivity that's keeping all of you entwined.

"It might also surprise you to know that despite all the negativity, she feels that remaining here with what's familiar must be better than where she fears she'll go when it's her time!"

This new perspective shifted the situation for my client. She was surprised to learn, *as many are*, that negative emotions are just as binding as positive ones. She was now motivated to do whatever she could to move from a frequency of hatred and angst to one of love and compassion. I felt that in time, this shift would help her mother let go.

This was the strongest I'd ever felt someone so tethered to the earth plane by all the negative reinforcement she was receiving from everyone in her life. It's fascinating how attached we become to our roles in the world, even when they haven't served us.

I recently received an update from the daughter that included confirmation about the way specific photos can open the heart:

Hi Louise! A portion of our consultation hit home for me because I had just taken a moment out of a very busy day to stop and look at an old family picture. It wasn't the one you picked up on, but one from 50 years ago. It showed my husband, his brother, and Mom & Dad, standing with an antique-looking cart and a herd of rather large pigs. Oddly I had stopped racing past the desk to pick up the picture and really look at it, not just dust it off, but really look at it and laughed out loud, and it opened my heart. But it wasn't a photo of my own mother.

Sometimes we're sent special moments to open our hearts.

It's always nice to receive confirmation from clients and witness them beginning to understand that there's much more at play than what we see on the surface. It's natural and human to feel cheated when life deals us tremendous challenges. Practicing reframing can help discharge some of those corrosive and anxious thoughts.

It might surprise you to find out that based on thousands of consultations I've done through the years, I'm confident that *we choose* the challenges we experience each lifetime.

Come on, Louise, I would NEVER choose this!

Here's the thing: the soul evolves by moving through challenges. Each lifetime, in turn, presents infinite opportunities to move beyond old beliefs and stumbling blocks that hold us back.

Try seeing your situation (perhaps your whole life) from your soul's perspective. Consider caregiving as an adventure in your soul's evolution. It's a revolutionary way of looking at your situation, but try it!

The heart remembers the good stuff.

TOOL #2: HOW TO GO BEYOND TIME: THE FISH HOOK TECHNIQUE

When you show up to care mindfully for yourself or others, you expand and *time expands*. In one story in the last chapter, a client's mother took me to the past. In another story, the client's wife transmitted a cosmic wink — a future moment.

AND believe it or not, there's a way *you* can transcend time — that is, to go beyond your usual, linear way of working with time.

Operating within prescribed timelines and tedious 'To Do' lists limits us, and increases stress. The Fish Hook Technique can bring about change and de-stress your days, typically filled with so many imposing obligations. I describe this technique and the history behind it on the Illuminations website:

I had returned to New York City, where I was living at the time, having been on the road for nearly three months. I saw on my schedule that my assistant had overbooked me with phone consultations the next day, my first full day back!

I was also scheduled to do a talk for a FIONS group (Friends of the Institute of Noetic Sciences) that evening at 6 pm. They were meeting in an old church on the Upper East Side. I'd have to get there from the West Village to present in less than 30 minutes during rush hour! Not an easy task.

My mind kicked into gear the instant I opened my eyes and began making a list, which was why I felt stressed. "You'll never make it," my linear mind chimed in. "It's too much to do in too little time." Then I remembered how my spirit operates more efficiently outside of time. I needed to set it free.

I took a deep breath and cleared my head. Then I mentally did a quick scan, an overview of everything I needed to accomplish that day as if putting all the items on my radar screen. I visualized little illuminated blips floating around on the screen, rather than a linear list on a piece of paper.

Then I let it all go; I released it as if letting go of a hot air balloon with all the items on the list inside the basket.

Then I time-traveled to the future.

I saw myself standing behind the podium before the audience. I was feeling refreshed, fully present, and ready to begin my presentation.

I felt the texture of the sleeve of my silk jacket on my arm, the one I'd already decided to wear. I smelled the musty smell of the old church where the meeting would take place. I looked out at the attentive and appreciative audience, waiting with anticipation for me to begin. I spent a few moments in all of these sensations.

I visualized myself casting out a fish hook to that precise moment at the talk, feeling accomplished at all I'd completed, the ease with which I'd arrived, and the excitement about sharing my talk with an appreciative audience.

Then I let go of my visualization and any attempt to write the script. I could now trust the infinite creativity of the Universe to reel me into that future moment. I began my day, focused and present in each moment.

I moved through what I'd first anticipated as an impossible day, accomplishing everything effortlessly and effectively. I even managed an extra task, stopping by the cleaners!

I'd carried no lists in my head; my spirit knew the plan. It guided me through entirely in the flow.

That evening, I found myself at the podium in the old church, standing before my audience. The bells began chiming six o'clock.

Suddenly, I felt that 'future' moment kick in, the one to where I'd time-traveled at 7:00 a.m. that morning. It was all there — the scents, the fabric on my skin, the attendees anticipating the talk. It wasn't exactly *how I had 'pictured' it, but the Universe's interpretation of my visualizations was undoubtedly accurate!*

Did I create that future moment by going beyond time? Or, was I simply tapping into that moment already existing in my orbit? I suppose it's a bit like the chicken-and-the-egg, hard to know which came first. Either way, it works!

Try Going to the Future

First, get yourself relaxed, and take a deep breath.

Next, do a scan of all you need to accomplish by the end of the day — or, say — by 5pm *at the end of the week.*

Your scan might include tasks involving the one you're caring for, or items you've put on hold in your personal life.

Really imagine yourself there. Perhaps you're relaxing in your favorite chair, or lying on the couch or your bed. Open up all your senses to experience your surroundings and the feeling of relief and satisfaction. Take a nice big, deep breath and enjoy all you've accomplished.

Come back to the present moment and visualize yourself tossing out an imaginary fishing line. See the hook digging in securely to that future moment.

Finally, release all those images, that future moment, and any expectations or agendas you have. *Leave those details up to the Universe.*

Woo-hoo!

When the moment arrives, consider all the unforeseen circumstances and remarkable synchronicities — *seemingly psychic timing of events* that have transpired. Notice — how they all came together so magically and pulled you into a natural flow, delivering you to this very moment!

Don't chase down those synchronicities — just observe and embrace the feeling of awesomeness!

Congratulations!

You've just created a decisive, positive future moment with the Fish Hook Technique, and cleared space in your consciousness for the Universe to fill in the details!

You're now Dancing with the Universe! You're allowing your Higher-Self (and unseen helpers) to choreograph events in infinite and creative ways.

With a little practice, you might find yourself having a new relationship with time.

Back To The Present . . .

We all have those days when we're operating at a lower frequency. I have them. Sometimes, it feels nearly impossible to pull myself out of a dark corner of doubt. I'm challenged to find a single positive thought or expression of gratitude.

Clients deeply entrenched in caring for loved ones report having days when they feel fearful, discouraged, and alone. Some even say they feel abandoned or forgotten by a Higher Power. We are never abandoned!

You, too, might have days when you feel disconnected, and sometimes more critical of yourself (and others) than you do on better days. Tap into your inner resouce!

You are energy. We are all energy. We oscillate at higher or lower frequencies depending upon our thoughts, our moods, and our perspectives at any given moment.

We can adjust our frequency by consciously shifting our thinking from thoughts that make us feel fear or despair, to those that open our hearts and make us feel connected to those we care for, to others (even strangers), and to greater forces that guide, protect, and watch over us.

How do we do this? *Practice.*

Observe the moments when you're caught in obsessive thought loops about your situation, or find yourself trying to manage what's simply out of your control.

Feeling powerless can lead to anxiety, distraction, or lack of focus. It can also cause sleep disruption.

In those difficult moments, you have a choice. You can hang out in the discomfort of overwhelm, which feeds upon itself and spirals downward — or, you can observe what you're feeling and actively transform it.

To take one step out of the feeling into *observing* the feeling will give you the space to choose to respond in a better way. Observe that feeling.

It might help to say to yourself, "Well, this is an interesting feeling." Just that tiny, non-judgmental observation stops the downward spiral. Now you have the space to move into gratitude. How? *With one singular thought of being grateful.*

Grateful for the sunny day. Grateful that the traffic light is green. Grateful that your pet (or partner) is happy to see you! Grateful that you can laugh at yourself. *Anything.*

Spend time with this one thought of gratitude until it starts to expand and leads to other thoughts of gratitude. Note how *thoughts* of gratitude lead to *feelings* of gratitude. Allow this feeling to fill your whole body.

Then allow this expanse of gratitude to lift you up and teach you new things about yourself.

The more you practice gratitude, the more gratitude will begin to seek you out. You may be pleasantly surprised how gratitude will find you in unsuspecting moments.

— And Finally —

I'm so grateful for you and for the ways you're showing up in the world. Lean on tools in this book, and return to your Caregiver's Corner to ground yourself. Invite your Higher-Self to join the party and begin to experience your situation in new ways.

It is my greatest pleasure to work with caregivers and those you care for.

You are a courageous champion!

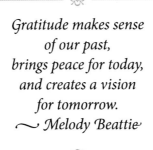

*Gratitude makes sense
of our past,
brings peace for today,
and creates a vision
for tomorrow.*
~ *Melody Beattie*

Love and Connection in Times of Uncertainty

I started writing *I'm Still In Here* in late 2019, before the advent of the World Pandemic of 2020. The difficulties of distancing from those we love, and the deep, collective grief for all the losses is like nothing we've experienced together before. But we're also more connected to one another, as we watch — and are deeply affected by — events unfolding in our global community.

All of my work, including the focus of my earlier books, has been geared toward helping folks understand that we are so much more than physical beings occupying our respective spaces on Planet Earth. We are boundless, and expand far beyond the limitations of our bodies. Everything in this book also applies to the current Pandemic crisis, and to unforeseen challenges that may lie ahead, any circumstances that might separate us in various ways from one another.

Space perceived as existing between us is just that — a *perception*. Our real work lies in closing that perceived gap. We *can* reach loved ones who seem unreachable. *And they can reach us*. It's all a matter of finding stillness and connecting through love...on the heart frequency.

There is no separation where there is love.

What I do want to impress upon readers of this book is that we MUST double down on self-care to better respond to all that we're dealing with in these times — and in times ahead. We must do what we can to stay healthy and present, to meet life right where it is, and stay out of fear, which cuts us off from finding new approaches to overcoming obstacles.

Out of trying times, incredible resourcefulness, creativity, and innovation can arise — the unifying evolution we've all been awaiting. Show up every day and keep expanding your personal practice. Continue sending out your unique positive energy into the world. Find gratitude wherever you can. Let's do our part to help the planet evolve!

Moving more into our truth, authenticity, and compassion will, in turn, deepen our metaphysical gifts. We just have to keep reminding ourselves that there's a bigger plan at play here, no matter what challenges we face together. We have to be willing to let go of old ways and expectations and embrace this time of uncertainty. At the other end of this is a new world, a better world. All for one, one for all.

Together, we'll look back and know that, indeed, hindsight is 2020.

Much Love,
Louise

I believe — that we're all in this together, here on Planet Earth, trying to find our way and maneuver on our paths the best we can. I personally believe our challenges are purposely and purposeFULLY amplified to make apparent the burdens we carry — the themes, attitudes, and issues we're here to resolve and move beyond.

Sometimes the way forward becomes clear when we surrender those burdens to a Higher Power, ask for guidance from wiser beings in our lives (or in the unseen), and enlist those with special talents who can help.

If you'd like assistance in helping you communicate with your loved one or assigned charge, I'm available for consultations.

email: louise@louisehauck.com
www.louisehauck.com

Made in the USA
Middletown, DE
10 March 2021